HAND-ME-DOWN HAIRCUT

Stevie Kilgour is a British–Irish poet from a council estate in Bedford. He gained his Doctorate in 2023 in Poetry, Masculinity and Working-class Studies. He believes in the power and importance of the working-class voice and its role in the creative industries. He didn't gain an education until he was 30 years old. He now spends his time in his kitchen in Leeds, drinking coffee and listening to 90s Jungle, drum and bass and metal. He supports Luton Town.

ISBN: 978-1-916938-59-5

Cover designed by Aaron Kent

Edited and Typeset by Aaron Kent

Broken Sleep Books Ltd
PO BOX 102
Llandysul
SA44 9BG

Contents

For Holly, everything is for you.
Create art, eat donuts, and drink good coffee.

For Sarah and my mum

Hand-me-down Haircut

Stevie Kilgour

Broken Sleep Books

Concrete, meet the working-class hooligan, a spirit uncontrolled / We carved out our sanctuary in the everyday struggles / The courage to embrace our truth / We were the silent revolutionaries / Carrying the torch of authenticity in the face of a society that often misunderstood our intentions in the shadow of our trainers / We were more than the sum of our DWP parts / we were bus stop warriors, champions of understanding / Keepers of our own narrative / We were working-class and gay / An embodiment of resilience and defiance pushing against a paradox / Some might say we were navigating a world where we held dimly lit rainbow aspirations / We were the sons and daughters living in a tapestry of muted colours and unspoken truths / We knew our worth lay in the strength of our resilience and not the weight of our wallets / Ignoring BBC voices and getting our bootleg copies from the back of a van at night / going to bed in our Sunday best and brand new Nike for fear they may be stolen from our home while our eyes are closed

When I was born I was a bulky mass
Of my mother's teenage rebellion
My cousin called me *an buachaill*
Spotty and identified like the bulk of four uncooked potatoes
Disappointment of blood and flat tyres which come only at knifepoint
On a council estate on peeling knees crawling out of English rain

I was birthed without friends or permission from any of the saints
Moist to the pith and
Re-gifted to my grandmother
Placed next to the constant never settling waves of Irish stew and
          boiling gammon
I stood beside my grandmother's kitchen pot alchemy in a cold
          Dublin kitchen
Her complexion wrinkled with the shadow of every wave on the Liffey

I wanted again to feel the happiness of growing slowly in the womb
Marinating in warmth up to my throat
A happy pulse clicking like tin heels on a dancefloor
Whipping with excitement I asked my grandmother in a way that
          only a grandson can;
When will I be ready?
My grandmother whispered; *tiocfiadh ár lá*
And I knew I should be careful to repeat that at school

For my Nan, my great grandparents
and all my Irish family

I'm Southern fried chicken

Running away from the things that lads do on holiday

I'm from halfway up the wooden hill to Bedfordshire

Full of the rising passion and rebellion of Irish family —

Ar aghaidh leis an éirí amach

Under milk teeth, I'm untroubled by the creeping clouds of maturity

I'll grow into this accent and the slang

My great grandfather, Patrick said *never sit with your back to the*
                    pub door

And *being known in the estates is just local Hollywood for poor people*

I wake each day with my morning hair full of takeaway grease /
My head sliding from the quiet happiness found in dreams where
I'm confident in a floral shirt / or the concentrated energy of
nightmares where I lose my genitals / I feel most at ease in a state of
consciousness where I watch the action of others / or myself moving
in and out of erratic rusted chainsaw motion / In these conscious
states my name is pronounced with the same involuntary smile a
mouth makes when it asks for strawberries / In those subconscious
states I punch with the efficiency of a Catholic mass at a rave / but
there is no violence until I'm attacked by a feral black dog / it rips
at my larynx and my thighs / I feel nothing because I'm a spectator
/ I don't die because dying can't happen / I'm needed elsewhere /
needed as a father / my greasy hair lumbering into participation
always being poor and late for the bus / always stinking with cheap
lager breath / washing up last night's arguments and my girlfriend
hates me / where is the dog / he's late

Violence is occurring

In the form of language

Being careful my mouth doesn't break my nose

Blood boiling from behind the bones in my chest

Breaking through the small indentation at the base of my neck

Did you know the word *Man* in Irish is translated as *Fear?*

Some violence now sits behind my forehead

In the form of expectation

An expectation of violence as a result of *Fear*

The last time the pain visited it was as stomach cramps

My fake dad breathed slowly for me

Precisely one year later to this exact moment

Beneath this same cloud

I had a cold shower

I craved like a slug the damp reassuring grey evening on concrete

A day with moist concrete and leaves

I hang around the avenue where my mother can see me

From the bedroom window, I watch a postcode battle

Curb-crawling antics of men in search of a pair of happy eyes

I fake cry and have no fight left

Absent from man-to-man talks

Flighty with the speed of every frightened song thrush

Looking for my fake dad from this bedroom window

Seeing him in shadows beside dog shit bushes

Waiting for the nod of his sober brow

My fake dad was the unattainable ruin

I remember the day I dug out a river
With my arms playing the role of
Perfect chandeliers lighting the length
Of my imperfect torso I believed I was a man with tough ligaments
The expulsion of power and whir from my sparrow wings
Purging my muscle and mucus to a point no boy should reach
Evicting sick-tired-looking colours from my cheekbones

My bedroom secrets keep me like a pig in my shit
My crackling skin under-lit to hide my invading misogyny
I'm surrounded by the illusion of vascular trees in a distressed
forest – (this council estate)
Each branch covering the burned heads of poor forgotten
children (me and my house)
I reach up to a lonely astronaut hiding in the shadow of the moon
I'm hopeful for a future of cash and successful biceps
I realise this is all a parade I'll always be a day late for the opening

How to rot an apple

Grasp it by the base of the neck

With Saturday night knuckles

Place it far from its family tree

Allow it to expire in a chair with Sunday's slow-face

With the blemish-free innocence and inexperience

Seen in new-born hands

Behind the eyes of the apple

Sits an immature core

Pale soft exposed

Drying out in the presence of a rough oak trunk

The bruises on my thighs are all the flat keys on a piano
I'm looking for that break in the sequence that might
Arrive timetabled in a key change or with friends knocking on the
        door
I'm fearful of my forced relationship with brass belt buckles
Scared my accent will burn the roof of my mouth
Or having to learn outdated dad voices
Afraid my sperm won't work and my drama could never be serialised
Panicked my Adam's apple will rot from the base
Terrified I'll have my jaw cracked like a bad joke
Wild birds migrate out of the postcode of me
Pulling away from the polite posture of my winter hair
I think about fashioning an unexceptional pair of wings
It will be made from lost pubic hair and day-old takeaway chicken
        bones
Hopeful of joining the birds and no longer having to taste cigarette
        ash and petrol

I place all my failures on the backs of common houseflies

I ask them all to join me in my adult bedroom

The room is packed to the electrics

The door could not be forced shut

I leave scared of the scene I manifested

The buzzing of silver wings growing uncontrollable

Drawing the attention of all the stepdads in the world

Linked at their high waist belt loops

All of them carrying their own uniquely rolled-up newspapers

In perfect syncopation to

The sound of my blood vessels and swelling fingers

Bulging dads in authoritative marching

War-like in drunken inner speculation of my antics

They are almost at the door

This hair dye could only hide me for twenty-eight washes

Scott moved out of the estate the day before Joe Strummer died

Scott's red brick house became a red brick Tesco Express

I would pass the red brick Tesco and look up at Scott's ex-bedroom
window

Scott took the good Play Station controller my milk teeth and our
accrued teenage wisdom

Scott moved out of the estate in 2002 the day of the Great
Conjunction of Aquarius

but I still go into that red brick house as it is now

Helping myself to the ice cream in the freezer

Whenever someone has a birthday I tell them *congratulations on the anniversary of the day you escaped the womb* / escaping must always be seen as an achievement even if we escape the smell and warmth of our mothers / our mothers celebrate these anniversaries with us celebrating with the same melancholy of the relay runner who is second for the baton / they win but they never cross the line for the glory and never get the gunshot anticipation at the beginning / we feel sorrow for our gentle mothers as we think this / I'm told that one day our mothers picked us up and put us down / and never picked us up again / beneath this revelation is a gentle sigh / a single exhaled note from behind my throat disguised as I gulp / marking the start of a song where I may finally be able to cry / I'm not even sure what we're celebrating anymore

I remember that day in the park when Kevin shouted; *you gay bro?*

In my head, I was *Holy Joe*

I executed the most beautifully perfect chewing gum volley

To the back of Kevin's shaved head

In all of this bravery and the romance of battle

I thought that was how love was born

I wrote it down in my diary

The ambition I cradled last night was to be an active volcano
My unmistakable nostrils flared on the dancefloor
My uncomplicated mouth mimicked the gasps from football terraces
I imagine spewing ash covered ants (& ants & ants & ants & ants)
Ants spilling onto the streets beyond two in the morning
Staying up to see the magpies arrive with the sun and the bin
        trucks in town
For the best part of two years, I have woken every day alone
Clutching a hangover in bed during prime church hours
Smoking and waiting for that receding hairline
I have counted through each day seeing my imprint darken with
        rust on the mattress
The ambition I cradle to today is to move as a hermit crab would
Move away from a sea of bottles
Move away from a beach-battered childhood
Begin to build a raft starting with the most beautiful sail

The shop window is decorated like bedrooms
I desired a brilliant white desk a brilliant white bedframe
A sign reading it's okay to rest and my fists unfold
All the missed Christmases crawling exhausted to my throat
The backs of my eyelids are graffitied
(I'm sorry Mum)
I am surrendering the inside of my trouser pockets
Showing brilliant white open palms
I step backwards off the curb away from
My functioning body made of animal proteins
Vacating the New Year
Appearing again in all twenty-three picture frames in the family
hallway

Sadness is happening

Our mothers are privately crying into the clean washing

In the garden

I'm strategically folding myself into fresh kindling

For the winter

Our family washing is always stained

I'm growing a new manhood / it'll soon spoil / sleep in my eyes / the pageant of biceps taken down like the flinching of sunflowers in winter / it may grow again next year to new lights and heat / my brother - a young cardinal his eyes full of sex-bed aromas in the small violent hours / a throbbing tongue boiling a promise alive every minute / medication swelling our joint jugulars / inheriting our great-grandfather's vascular anger at the 'Irish Problem' / still angry at famine with fists tight like the skin on the back of a runners knee / I return home to plait my daughter's knotty brown hair – which she gets from me / we paint our nails in rainbow happiness – which I get from her

My uncle has a rowdy friend

His presence is made of the skin on a cold cup of tea

I'm there posing in the shape of a horde of hesitant summer gnats

Releasing the pressure from my bruised scapula

The friend called me 'the little queer'

My slender torso ducking this customary masculine confrontation

/

I saw that man three FIFA World Cups later

Holding the business end of a hammer to his toes

Exposing the fragility of his shoulder blades

I abandoned my egg sandwich

It was only Monday

The cheap deodorant made me smell as fresh as un-chewed
            rainbow bubble gum

When a man dies his fists unclench

Violence relaxes its jaw

Cholesterol permeates younger soil

Can a man ever really separate himself from the aggressive?

Saturday night maybe a Sunday morning

I knew a man who once asked me to

Lay beside him and give it up

I didn't understand the importance of January on this man

His rib cage was half buried already the top of his heart was still
        kind of red

I saw this man as a faded young kite perforated and stuck in
        December's dead trees

None of this is real (ly about giving up)

I pulled out a chair and we talked about the lament of small birds

In branchless months he told me how he had a son once

The tears slipped from his face

Showed a reluctance to be spoken about

If I held my mother's hand

She held her mother's hand

She then held her mother's hand

And every one of us followed this process of discovery

We could meet again on the first day of school

Or amongst all the original cries of birth

Hands gripping the wire fences surrounding the playground

We could say things like *no, it'll be okay in the end*

Everything could smell like freshly turned soil

For Aisling

Every splinter I pull from my daughter's palm

Is god tearing telegraph poles from concrete

I only fit the fleeting description of a man

Being a father in profile

Rejecting emphatic blue English skies in summer

Wryly emptying my pockets of dull pennies

Taping over my faulty wiring and broken teeth

Living through amplified green moss on stones grey flowers and
        dead dragonflies

Visible only by the opening of a sewer hatch and the stinking
        dampness of winter

Away from the dirty backhand of my stepdad

Away from the sight of him spitting onto the hot side of the iron

The saliva raced away quicker than our battered mother

Now I'm standing in the sand pit

A ten-year-old boy in blue bottoms

Walking my ghosts to the swing set

Singing in pig grunts and ripped jeans

Dragging tired baggage under my eyes

Becoming *Holy Joe*

Holy Joe is low on cigs
Everything becoming the pink sour innards of a grapefruit
As he stuffs his pockets with all the trembling vibrations
From his sibling's lips
He'll give you something to fuckin' cry about
This is all done to the screech of
An ambulance on two wheels
Momentarily on a curb
And the garden gnomes didn't see anything
So don't fucking ask

**I want to unveil an online persona as large as any cathedral in
Barcelona**

Stained glass windows showing me on horseback pulling social
media posts from a scabbard

Over my violent shoulder is a saddle full of shit emojis and
prepared replies

For my absent dad and gazing Parisians their smiles are black smoke

By the way, I'm in Paris now looking for the right filter to impress
my ex-girlfriend

I'm invisible to her but still on top of her

Timeline still top of the first page on any search engine seeing her
in a bikini and

Remembering our shared yeast infection

My skin was sheathed long enough to grow a devil beard

In my dream the pills changed colour

Shape

Texture

Theme

One was a rusty hammer

Another was a bruised mango

A third one was a wingless Magpie

                                    Asking for a foot to end it all

One melted before it got to my tongue

Then you said you were sending healing light rays

My terror was distilled

The colours began to separate further

Becoming beautiful detached cottages beside lakes

And like you, I was then repossessed by nature

For Melissa Lee-Houghton

I have waited ten whole football seasons

I no longer understand how affection occurs

Being told to smile or wait quietly outside The Howling Man

Feelings are a luxury few boys can afford

We all get the shit kicked out of us

In our dreams

I shut my eyes so tight it all goes black

Waking up to the smell of my stepdad's heat

Being told not to sob

Existing in blood and freckles

Holy Joe is occurring again
Wants the £1.20 in our pockets
Your mum is a slag, I could be your dad
He wants to put our lights out
Lay us down at the ankle of an
Oak tree
We study the clouds to recognise
Our location in anticipation of waking after the knockout
All this happens to the sound of tobacco
Moving into our lungs
Worms massaging our cheeks to rouse us
To spring to life and scream
From the protruding tongue of my four-stripe Adidas

Choosing my dad

From a conveyor belt of men in denim

Each of them grinding their wisdom teeth

Towards the back of the head of the next

Each father is an algorithm

Modelled on celebrated FA Cup-winning captains of the nineties

A version of myself arrives late

Slumped at the end of the line sucking on a dummy bleeding from
        the groin

Not concerned with the pursuit of brilliance

Underserving and composed of archaic childlike features

My mother walks away in black disappointment

I'm complicit with the shadow and the frown which resides where
        her face should be

This version of me is wrapped in day-old chip shop paper

Council estate tan

Hubcap Frisbee champion of Bedford

I'm the size of a cow

I'm the size of four cows in the month of August

Ruminating on concrete

Hoping to outgrow my shadow

Avoiding all the sleepovers

Watching men on the verge

Coping in torn school trousers

Acting soldier shaped only five minutes from home

Fake poisoning the stream that feeds the swans in town

If I wait here long enough maybe the neighbour's broken window
              will fix itself

If my mum asks where I was

I'll say I was picking wildflowers for the house

Holy Joe is stubbing a cigarette out on a phone box window

Takes the piss out of the neighbours

Invites them round for beer and a fire

The kids will be OK on their own – they're only next door

Might get a gram or two

Says he's a black belt in _No-Can-Do_

Belly laughs and blows smoke

Can get rid of your fridge for two notes – knows a local field

White collar boxer

All about the United on Saturday

Adidas Samba on – fake Stone Island

Home fans only pub

Have you met my mate Stanley?

Hoy Joe pulls out a blade

Finding condoms when we never used protection

My ex-girlfriend brought her new boyfriend home for protection I
said   oh
The day the wind blew my shed roof away with an   oh
The noises coming from my body are mostly made of weeping
and
The letters I write myself are those of condolence and blame
oh
The eyelids I prop open are fodder for television shows at
midnight
Excremental piety my guts yapping with sounds like   oh
While I think of the bonding of their privates   which
sounds like   oh
At times this slow destruction felt cathartic

I'm advancing out of recognition

Out of the identified roles, my dad agreed with bashed clocks and
        supermarket vodka

Away from customary firm handshakes and prick-waving

Slipping from the backseats of hot-boxed cars

No longer with friends In November in a McDonald's car park

Laying in on a Sunday regretting the dirty text to Natalie

Finding cheering crowds and blossoms brightly lit but not for me

Building a covenant between the body and the heaviest of stones
        but not for me

I'm going to buy a mirror so I can watch myself starve in 'hand-
        me-down' trousers

Holy Joe has his arms folded now

Overlooking two men spit in cuss words

Knows he could take both

If he wanted

One man is choking the other now

Another man's girlfriend is crying about how purple he has turned

The shadows which emanate from all the men I've known

Visibly made up of the frailty of poorly settled jelly

The futile fight of a single ice cube sat in grandad's whiskey

Tasting just the same as the weakness which comes from seeing

Your blood or vomit

For the first time

Each river surges with catholic guilt

There is a finite volume of water my legs can resist

Before being reduced to a water bead

Some men can't help but move with the swell

Feeling the current of each day's venom my the ribcage

The trees which bear fruit watch me in the stream

Offering a branch to pull me from the wake

A rotten disease beneath the surface allowing them to snap in my grasp

Holy Joe breathes heavily with
Heart disease
Once de-gloved his muddied hand
Waits for Yasser to finish praying
Before he lays him out like a Pakistani rug
Speaks for the entire island
Bacardi-geezer
Rest your head on the concrete pillow
The estate hums along with the pylons
Something about August makes the
Boys buzz like electricity

I had that dream again
    (Poem)

The one where I plan my funeral
    (Poem)

The correct car arrives with all the relevant flowers and I'm smoking
Driven toward a changing of the guard
    (Poem)

In the back seat a mortician considerately chips away at my front
    teeth
I lower the window and watch an ambling grey feather drop
    gently into my lap
I'm reduced to bleeding gums and exposed pulp
    (Poem)

My chest is open now and I'm sick/nervous

I inspect the gaping holes in my mouth with an Argos pencil
    (Poem)

When I woke the location had changed again
It's my birthday and I am considering going wild on a rope
    (Poem)

My partner gives me a card scrawled with a blood-red heart
I look out of the bedroom window matching my breaths to the
    flow of the wind
Decapitating a field of dandelions
    (Poem)

There were happy days in spite of rain / bushes surfed by cousins / the warmth offered up by mossy mattresses / chasing foxes at three AM / being chased by cops at three PM /shadow boxing in the park / buying all the chicken legs in the takeaway / being four nil down but next goal wins / jumping the neighbours fence / the Rottweiler wants my ankles as chew toys / stolen mopeds ridden once and abandoned / no school even during term time / my nan and her Irish traveller rage at the local shop sign reads / NO BLACKS NO DOGS NO IRISH / she was constantly gasping for a brew and spitting feathers / by eighteen I'll be rich / by twenty two I'll be rich / by twenty seven I'll be rich / lying to myself every five years / drunk and skunk then sick all day / at nineteen shagged a bird / at twenty nine fucked a bitch / at thirty nine made love to my beautiful fiancé / trying to grow emotionally / tea party with my daughter / no longer caring about who sees me only lift 20kg in the gym / rewiring the plugs / patriarchy weight is heavy / no longer wearing masks / it still rains but there is no spite / full of delayed bereavement / putting up crushed velvet wallpaper / baby kicks / the hems of my trouser legs sit flush now against the tolerant shine of my shoes / and we can call this a transformation of sorts

The rhythm of trainers slapping against concrete / this shin slapping some other boy about / unapologetic / second skin— trackies / hoodie pulled tight / local shop / clenched fist discount / laughing with mates while foxes fuck in bins and bushes / your neighbour's number plates - my bedroom wall / my chin jutted forward - your neighbour calling the cops because they can smell it / there is a person behind this stereotype / but he's no more endearing than then visible façade / I'm both the mask I wear and the face beneath it in an endless contradiction of 100 % street beef and peace / *The Troubles* are at home too / it's hard to think of love and forget the money when the money lives next door and doesn't want to hang out and love popped out for bread and milk thirty years ago and never returned

Acknowledgements

Thank you Aaron Kent and all associated with Broken Sleep Books for being an inspiration. Thank you, Melissa Lee-Houghton for your support, and Bobby Parker, Wayne Holloway-Smith, and Christopher Lloyd for their guidance and advice in writing these poems.

I owe so much to my mum, Teresa, Sarah Hutt, Daniel Ardis, Aisling Goodwin, my Nan, Jane Yates, the memory of Barry Yates and my beautiful daughter Holly Nola Kilgour.

To all my family in the UK, all those who brought me up and grew up with me, my amazing relatives in Ireland, and all the roots and branches of the Donohoe tree, those we have lost over the years and the ones we share drinks with now, this is for you. Go raibh maith agat.

Working-class laughs and struggles, British birth, rebellious Irish heart. Mum's hugs, Nan's stew, stout with Len, coffee with Trudy, late night drives, Jason, Lisa Growing up in pubs, being in bands – James Straker, and Mike Hutt for letting me use his house in the Dales to finish edits. For Dublin, Bedford, Leeds, Big Mick Harford, Padraig Pearse, Pelly Ruddock Mpanzu, Metal, Indie, Jungle, Drum and Bass, Grindcore Cake Makers and Luton Town Football Club – Come on you Hatters!

LAY OUT YOUR UNREST

www.ingramcontent.com/pod-product-compliance
Lightning Source LLC
LaVergne TN
LVHW041237080426
835508LV00011B/1262